Contents

Contents

Series preface

Whether you are a tutor/trainer or studying management development to further your career, Super Series provides an exciting and flexible resource to help you to achieve your goals. The fifth edition is completely new and up-to-date, and has been structured to perfectly match the Institute of Leadership & Management (ILM)'s new unit-based qualifications for first line managers. It also harmonizes with the 2004 national occupational standards in management and leadership, providing an invaluable resource for S/NVQs at Level 3 in Management.

Super Series is equally valuable for anyone tutoring or studying any management programmes at this level, whether leading to a qualification or not. Individual workbooks also support short programmes, which may be recognized by ILM as Endorsed or Development Awards, or provide the ideal way to undertake CPD activities.

For learners, coping with all the pressures of today's world, Super Series offers you the flexibility to study at your own pace to fit around your professional and other commitments. You don't need a PC or to attend classes at a specific time – choose when and where to study to suit yourself! And you will always have the complete workbook as a quick reference just when you need it.

For tutors/trainers, Super Series provides an invaluable guide to what needs to be covered, and in what depth. It also allows learners who miss occasional sessions to 'catch up' by dipping into the series.

Super Series provides unrivalled support for all those involved in first line management and supervision.

Unit specification

Title:	Giving briefings and making presentations in the workplace	Unit Ref:	M3.09
Level:	3		
Credit value:	1		

Learning outcomes	Assessment criteria	
The learner will	*The learner can (in an organization with which the learner is familiar)*	
1. Know how to conduct a briefing/ presentation	1.1	Select appropriate information in line with the objectives of the briefing or presentation
	1.2	Logically structure the content of the briefing/presentation
	1.3	Introduce an appropriate management topic clearly
	1.4	Use appropriate presentation techniques and aids to enhance understanding of the topic of briefing/presentation
	1.5	Present information clearly
	1.6	Display confidence in the subject matter
	1.7	Keep to time
	1.8	Use feedback to check understanding
	1.9	Design a simple evaluation form

Workbook introduction

1 ILM Super Series study links

This workbook addresses the issues of *Giving Briefings and Making Presentations in the Workplace*. Should you wish to extend your study to other Super Series workbooks covering related or different subject areas, you will find a comprehensive list at the back of this book.

2 Links to ILM qualifications

This workbook relates to the learning outcomes of Unit M3.09 *Giving briefings and making presentations in the workplace* from the ILM Level 3 Award, Certificate and Diploma in First Line Management.

3 Links to S/NVQs in management

This workbook relates to the following Unit of the Management Standards which are used in S/NVQs in management, as well as a range of other S/NVQs:

B6. Provide leadership in your area of responsibility.

4 Workbook objectives

Speaking in public is high on most people's list of things they dread most. The image of all those faces staring at us and waiting for a brilliant display or rhetoric is enough to make us weak at the knees. But it needn't be like that. By following a few simple rules and doing a great deal of practice, you can master the skills needed to communicate confidently and with authority.

Session A of this workbook helps you to develop your communication skills so that you will be able to deliver clear and effective briefings to members of your team and others in your work environment. It will show you how important it is to plan what you are going to say and how you are going to say it. It also emphasizes the value of using visual aids to support your presentation.

Session B supports this by showing how you can use present information to make it easier to understand using tables, charts and diagrams. It will also show you how you can use software tools such as spreadsheets to produce charts that are clear and easy for others to interpret.

4.1 Objectives

When you have completed this workbook you will be better able to:

- Prepare and deliver effective briefings to your team, and contribute to briefings given by others.
- Select the most appropriate way to present statistical information.
- Present charts and diagrams effectively.
- Interpret statistical information from tables, charts or diagrams.

5 Activity planner

You may decide to look at the following activities now:

- For Activity 4 you need to enlist a friend or colleague to listen to a short briefing you have prepared.
- Activity 13 requires you to attend a briefing given by someone else.
- Activity 20 requires you to make a video recording of a briefing you have prepared, if possible.

Activities 6 to 9 and Activity 20 may provide the basis of evidence for your S/NVQ portfolio. All Portfolio Activities and the Work-based assignment are sign-posted with this icon.

The icon states the elements to which the Portfolio Activities and Work-based assignment relate.

Session A
Successful briefings and presentations

▪ 1 Introduction

A rumour had been circulating all afternoon that something was about to happen. People were getting nervous. Then word went round that everyone should congregate in the programming team's work area. There was going to be a briefing. The contractors weren't sure whether they were included as well as the permanent staff, but they went anyway.

Neil, the team leader, cleared his throat and, with his eyes fixed firmly on the floor, announced that their project had been cancelled and there would be redundancies. That was all he could say until more details had been decided. Everyone spent the rest of the afternoon in little worried huddles, wondering what was going to happen next.

This was a bad experience for everyone involved, and they all blamed Neil. Indeed, he had very little going for him – no hard facts, no backup from his superiors, no good news to soften the below. But even in this extreme situation he could have handled the situation much better.

In this session you will learn how to present information – whether good or bad – so that everyone will come away from the briefing with an understanding of your message and a feeling that they have been fully informed.

2 The purpose of briefings and presentations

The main purpose of briefings and presentations is to:

- give information out;
- get information back.

There are several situations in which you may have to give a briefing or presentation, for example:

- telling your team about some change that will affect them – as Neil was attempting to do in the example above;
- getting all team members to share information about their work in progress;
- informing a group of visitors about some aspect of your work;
- updating senior managers on team progress.

Activity 1

4 mins

What briefings or presentations have you attended recently, either as the presenter of the information or as part of the audience? List three of them.

_____

_____

_____

Briefings and presentations can be a pleasure, a necessity, a chore, a nuisance or a test, depending on the circumstances.

They can seem like a waste of valuable time. They certainly take up time; many briefings are badly organized and poorly run. They can be inconclusive and frustrating. Depending on your past experience, you may strongly dislike them.

But briefings and presentations are a fact of every manager's life; the point is to learn to make them work, and not to hold too many because, if they are seen as time-wasters, they will lose their impact and people will eventually not even bother to attend.

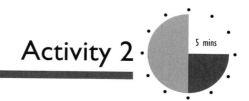

Activity 2

Think back to some of the less successful briefings and presentations you have attended in the past. Write down five or six words that describe what you felt was wrong with them.

_____

_____

_____

You may have suggested that they were too long, they dealt with trivia, you couldn't hear all that was said, they were badly presented or they concerned matters that were irrelevant to your own work.

However, a briefing or presentation doesn't have to be like that. It can be efficient, productive and even enjoyable as long as you:

■ prepare for it carefully;
■ ensure that your audience is also prepared;
■ conduct it effectively.

3 Which medium?

Briefings can be delivered verbally or in writing.

3.1 Verbal briefings and presentations

Formal verbal briefings and presentations are highly structured, and communication is often more one way than it is in an informal briefing. Examples include:

■ presentations given to external groups to explain the activities of your work area;
■ regular 'tool box talks' to your team members about some aspect of their work.

Informal verbal briefings are usually briefings which you give to your team when you want to:

- bring about changes of attitude or behaviour;
- co-ordinate team actions;
- explain something new.

Every time you brief members of your team you are also affecting the way they relate to one another. Since these are working relationships, this incidental aspect of communication is important.

Even the most casual and 'off the record' chat can help to:

- mould attitudes;
- strengthen team spirit;
- show you and the team members where you stand in relation to one another.

Activity 3

2 mins

David calls his team together and explains that the Chief Executive Officer (CEO) of the whole corporate group will be visiting the site tomorrow.

What purpose does this briefing serve?

_____

_____

What effects is it likely to have on the team's working relationships?

_____

_____

There are two purposes behind this simple communication: an **open** agenda and a **hidden** agenda.

The open agenda is about practical objectives – in this case to inform the team members about the CEO's visit so that they will be prepared for it.

Information is empowering.

The hidden agenda is about feelings and attitudes – keeping the team informed encourages trust and team spirit. It also helps the individual team members to feel more involved in events, and hence more empowered.

If David's communication hits its target, the world is changed in three small but useful ways:

- the team members possess some information they didn't have before;
- they have the choice to take action, for example, to tidy their desks;
- their confidence in the team leader is strengthened.

The meaning of this for you as a manager should be obvious. When you speak to your team members:

- you often do so in order to achieve a particular objective;
- you always affect the way they relate to you.

If you brief your team well, you can strengthen bonds, create loyalty, build morale and improve productivity. If you brief them poorly, or not enough, the opposite can happen.

3.2 Written briefings

If you work in a large organization you are probably familiar with the emailed 'Message from the CEO' which arrives at regular intervals in your mailbox. They are often full of information which appears to be totally irrelevant to you, but if you read them you may learn more about how your organization works.

Written communication is usually much more formal than verbal communication.

To see the difference, you only need to write down word for word what someone says. It will usually look very disjointed in print.

In the last few years more and more written briefings have been distributed in the form of emails. They can range from being one-line reminders to long-winded communications that most people tend to ignore. It is left up to the recipients whether to download them to a PC or to print them out. There is usually no way that the sender can tell that the message has been received.

The advantage of writing is that we usually have longer to absorb it. Spoken words are gone almost instantly.

In general, it is preferable to communicate in writing when the briefing:

- is a short, non-controversial message (often sent via email);
- is long and relatively complicated;
- contains background information and supporting documentation;
- doesn't involve changing the team members' attitudes or feelings.

The rest of this session will concentrate on the skills required to give verbal briefings, although most of the rules also apply to written ones. In Session B we will look at some of the issues that arise in presenting written briefings specific.

4 Selecting information

In selecting the information to present at your briefing session or presentation, you need to think about the following questions:

- what sort of people are in my audience?
- what are the **key** facts and feelings I want to pass on to them, i.e. what are my objectives?
- what do they know already?
- what are their current attitudes and feelings?

How much do you know about your audience? If they are your team members, then you probably have a pretty good idea about how much they know and feel. If they are visitors to the organization or members of another department, you can't assume very much at all. If this is the case, there are three simple rules for what you say and how you say it:

- don't assume your listeners know as much as you do;
- don't use language they might not understand;
- don't give them too much information too quickly.

4.1 Don't make assumptions

Activity 4 · 15 mins

You need a colleague or friend to help in this Activity – someone who is not an electrical specialist. Ask him or her to sit quietly and listen carefully. Then slowly read out this extract from a technical lecture.

'As the magnets rotate, a pole passes the ignition chargecoil, which generates a current through the rectifier R1. This charges up the capacitor to a voltage of, say, 350 volts; the magnet rotates further and generates a pulse of electrical energy in a "pulse coil". The coil is movable around the stator, so that timing may be adjusted. The energy pulse passes through the rectifier R2 to the gate of the thyristor, whereupon the thyristor conducts, and the stored electrical energy in the capacitor gives a high, short-duration current through the ignition coil primary. The secondary voltage produces a plug spark in which the "rise time" is extremely short, a condition which will make the plug work well, even though it may have an incorrect gap or be partly fouled. You can think of this sudden discharge as punching a way through the plus fouling salt deposits. Note the absence of a contact breaker in this form of CDI.'

Now ask your colleague these three questions:

1 What is this passage describing?

2 How is the capacitor charged?

3 How can the timing be adjusted?

If your colleague answers the questions correctly, it will be a remarkable performance. The vast majority of people would not be able to (unless they made detailed notes) because:

- there is too much information;
- too much of it is new;
- it is too complex;
- it uses technical language with which most people would not be familiar.

Any listener who can make sense of it must:

- already have a lot of knowledge of the subject;
- understand technical jargon such as 'stator' and 'rise time'.

Do you only brief people who know as much about your subject as you do? Probably not. Often your listeners will be other first line managers and their teams, trainees, visitors and people from other departments.

4.2 Information overload

First tell them what they MUST know, then what they SHOULD know, and finally, and only if you have the time, what they COULD know.

A speaker who overloads the audience with information is wasting everybody's time. All listeners have a limit: they can soak up what they hear, but only so much and only so fast.

In practice, if you give your listeners too much information too quickly:

- some of it will not get through at all;
- some of it will get through in a mangled or muddled state;
- you will have no idea what has got through correctly and what hasn't;
- if you really overdo it, your audience may give up listening altogether.

Activity 5 · 3 mins

Given the example in Activity 4 and the comments above, how can you avoid giving your listeners information overload? Make a note of at least **five** things you can do.

_____

_____

_____

_____

_____

Answers can be found on page 82.

If you follow these rules, you will benefit in two ways:

- you will need to say less;
- more of it will get through.

4.3 Dealing with sensitive issues

When you are selecting the material for your briefing or presentation, keep in mind the impact it might have on your audience. It is always useful to be forewarned of any opposition that might arise during your briefing. In sensitive situations (such as announcements of cut-backs or work reorganization), use your contacts to find out who might be particularly hostile as well as who might be particularly friendly.

Once you have identified such people you can try to help the situation by:

- sending round papers or memos explaining your case;
- using your network to discover the nature of their objections;
- lobbying – explaining your case and asking for support on a one-to-one basis;
- doing deals – agreeing to support another person's case in return for their supporting yours.

Your preparatory work will help you to put over your argument at the meeting itself.

5 Planning and preparation

If you have prepared your briefing or presentation thoroughly, you will have every reason to feel confident when you actually give it. But you must be prepared to put in the effort – most speakers find that they **spend at least five times longer preparing a briefing than they actually spend giving it.**

A well tried formula for preparing a briefing is as follows:

Step	Action
1	Draft the objectives
2	List the content
3	Design the structure
4	Prepare visual aids and demonstrations
5	Have a rehearsal

Let's look at each step in detail.

5.1 Step 1: Draft the objectives

Think about your purpose, the needs of your listeners and the context in which you will be giving the briefing. Ask yourself:

■ what is the purpose of the briefing or presentation?
■ who will be listening?
■ where will I be doing the briefing or presentation?

When you are clear about the answers to these questions, write down your objectives for the briefing, i.e. what you want the audience to be able to do as a result. For example:

> Suppose you have to give a briefing to a group of local secondary school teachers who are considering placing work-experience students with your organization. They want to know what it is like to work in your team, and the sort of work you actually do. The briefing will take place at the Teachers' Centre, and you will have up to 15 minutes altogether, plus a little time for questions.

Your main objective might be:

'by the end of the briefing the secondary school teachers will be able to accurately describe the work done by my team'.

5.2 Step 2: List the content

Decide the key points you need to put across to your audience in order to achieve your objectives.

Activity 6

Using a separate sheet of paper make a list of the key points you would want to make. This Activity may provide the basis of appropriate evidence for your S/NVQ portfolio.

5.3 Step 3: Design the structure

Work out a sensible and logical structure for the points you are going to make. This should consist of:

- an introduction;
- a main part;
- an end (summary and conclusions).

Always design the main part first.

Main part

This is where you expand and explain the key points listed in step 2. For example, if your first point is that your organization has 'a reputation for quality', you may want to support that by stating:

- who thinks so;
- what you mean by quality;
- why it is considered important;
- what you do to maintain it.

Let's work out a way of putting down the content of a briefing, using the example already given above. Look back at the details of the briefing to the teachers outlined in section 5.1.

Now let's look at how you can develop the main message.

Activity 7

S/NVQ B6

This Activity, together with Activities 8 and 9, may provide the basis of appropriate evidence for your S/NVQ portfolio.

Look back to your response to Activity 6 and, building on that, think again carefully about what you need to say. If you need to change anything, do so. Then write down on a separate sheet of paper the main points again in logical order as briefly as you can. Choose no more than **eight** key points.

When you are happy with your list of key points, write each one at the top of a blank sheet of paper or large index card. These will be the skeleton of your briefing.

Now you need to go through the process of refining each key point to include everything else you need to mention. The result will be a list of subsidiary points under each key point.

Activity 8

S/NVQ B6

This Activity, together with Activities 7 and 9, may provide the basis of appropriate evidence for your S/NVQ portfolio.

Consider each of your key points in turn and list under each one the subsidiary points, making sure you put them in logical order.

For example:

KEY POINT	I	A REPUTATION FOR QUALITY
SUBSIDIARY POINTS	1.1	Operating at quality end of the market
	1.2	Customers are very demanding (reject anything not to highest standard)
	1.3	Competition intense; quality keeps customers loyal
	1.4	Highly skilled workforce
	1.5	Have made big investment in training (give examples)
	1.6	Rigorous inspection at every stage

You now have a complete skeleton of the main part of your briefing, written out in logical order on separate sheets or cards. This simple outline can be the basis of the visual aids that you will produce later.

Introduction, summary and conclusion

Activity 9 · 10 mins

S/NVQ B6

This Activity, together with Activities 6, 7 and 8, may provide the basis of appropriate evidence for your S/NVQ portfolio.

I   Take a clean sheet of paper or index card and head it INTRODUCTION.

2   Below that write down, as briefly as you can, the various things you need to say in your introduction to the teachers.

If you start by drafting the main body of the breifing, the introduction, summary and conclusion will practically write themselves.

For example:

INTRODUCTION

Good morning, etc.

My name is . . . . .

I am a first line manager at . . . .

We produce control systems

Up-to-date, high tech, forward looking

Stop me if there is anything

Happy to answer questions afterwards.

---

3   Now use new sheets or cards to do the same for the summary and conclusion.

The conclusion needs a little thought. Think about what this particular group of listeners needs to know, for example:

- your attitude to work experience students;
- what will be expected of them;
- what the students can expect to gain from the experience.

Activity 10
5 mins

Look at the following examples of introductions and conclusions and jot down whether you think each of them is good, or not, and why you think so.

1   'Well, I – um – as you know, I haven't done much of this speaking so I – um – can't promise to do anything too amazing. But, as I've been called on to say a few words about my section – component assembly – well here goes . . .'

_____

_____

2   'For the last six months we have been working (25 hours a day sometimes) on the Delta project. As the section team leader, I'd like to explain a bit about . . .'

_____

_____

3   'I am delighted to have the chance to share with you some of the good news we have had lately on the progress of the migration project. As you know, I am not one to boast about the achievements of my team, but I can't help pointing out . . .'

_____

_____

4   'Well, I think that's about all . . . Yes, I think so. That's it then.'

_____

_____

5   'So the main thing is for us to keep up the same level of work in the next financial year. And for that we need your support. Thank you.'

_____

_____

You may have said something along the following lines.

Speaker 1
Bad. Listening to this, you might sympathize with his nervousness, but you wouldn't be impressed. If you say you're not going to be any good, listeners will tend to believe you. Don't apologize for yourself. By the time you stand up to speak you are committed, so you might as well make the best of it.

This speaker is rather slow to get going. We don't know anything about what he is going to talk about, only that the self-confidence to do it is lacking. It would be better to get to the point straight away as Speaker 2 does.

Speaker 2
Good. The speaker gets to the point straight away and makes a slight joke ('25 hours a day sometimes') to establish a friendly relationship with the listeners.

Speaker 3
Good. This gets to the point in a friendly way and immediately gets listeners on the speaker's side ('I am delighted to . . . share with you . . .').

The performance is confident – the speaker makes a slight joke of the fact that she never boasts – and doesn't apologize for herself.

Speaker 4
Not very good. In the same way as you don't want to start to speak with an apology for yourself, so you don't want to finish by just letting your subject peter out. You can throw away a good, well-organized briefing by such a feeble

> Don't worry about the odd 'um' and 'er' – that's something everybody does.

ending. This is why it is often useful to include in your notes exactly what you want the last line to be. Quite frequently, your listeners won't even know that you have missed out part of what you intended to say if you finish with a flourish.

Speaker 5
Good. This is much better than Speaker 4. The speaker repeats the main point of the speech very briefly ('the main thing for us is to keep up the same level of work . . .') and leaves his listeners in no doubt about what is wanted from them.

And, having finished, the speaker stops – without any vague remarks about this being the end.

Notice, too, that the speaker thanks the listeners at this point. If you feel it is appropriate to thank your audience for their response, then this is the time to do it – at the end.

So we can now draw up a checklist of do's and don'ts to bear in mind when you come to do the briefing:

- don't apologize for yourself;
- do get to the point as soon as possible;
- don't just peter out – finish firmly;
- do thank your audience at the end if this is appropriate;
- if you are rattled, don't show it – just pause and take your time to sort it out;
- show them you're in charge, and do what has to be done: that's what the audience expects.

5.4 Step 4: Prepare visual aids and demonstrations

I hear and I forget.
I see and I remember.

There are excellent reasons for using diagrams, slides, models or other equipment that will help your listeners get the message because:

- they help your listeners to remember the points you are making;
- they make the whole presentation more interesting and credible;
- some things are easier to communicate visually than verbally.

Activity 11

4 mins

What kinds of visual aid would be useful in a briefing about your own work? Note down **four** different kinds.

_____

_____

_____

_____

Every situation will be different, but you could think about how to show the audience:

- what the working environment is like (slides, photos, perhaps a video);
- what the 'end product' is (actual examples, models, photos);
- what the work you do consists of (diagrams, charts, samples);
- how the workload, output, etc. has progressed (diagrams, charts).

Visual aids don't have to be graphical, of course. One of the most useful things to do is to 'flash up' your key points in writing as you go along – on a flipchart, as slides for an overhead projector (OHP) or as a projected 'PowerPoint' demonstration.

For example, if your first key point is 'This company has always had a reputation for quality', you could present it on the OHP or flipchart page like this:

A reputation for quality

You could then keep that point on view until you are ready to make the next point. Alternatively you could put all your points on one sheet or slide and talk through them one by one.

EXTENSION 1
This extension gives you a brief guide to using overhead projectors and other visual aids.

Visual aids are extremely useful but they need careful preparation, so make sure you allow yourself enough time. Good visual aids can make your presentation go better, but if they are torn, scruffy, smudged or hard to see, it will go worse. In Session B, we will look at how you present numerical information clearly as part of your briefing or presentation.

Before you begin your presentation, remember to check that:

■ all your visual aids are ready;
■ the equipment is set up and working properly.

**I hear and I forget.
I see and I remember.
I do and I understand.**

Sometimes, if you are doing a team briefing, you might want to demonstrate rather than just talk. For example, a new method for disposing of waste packing materials might involve you in:

■ walking the team round the site, and pointing out examples of good and bad practice;
■ demonstrating how to use a machine designed to compress waste into bundles – a potentially dangerous machine.

There is a standard formula for this kind of briefing:

1	Introduce the subject and describe what is required.
2	Explain why.
3	Explain when the new procedure is to be used.
4	Demonstrate how to carry out the procedure.
5	Ask team members to do it for themselves.
6	Correct and advise them where necessary.
7	Check understanding and competence.
8	If necessary, repeat steps 4 to 7.

5.5 Step 5: Have a rehearsal

You should now have a set of up to ten sheets or cards, most of which should not have very much written on them, and a set of visual aids.

Most of the hard work is behind you. You have created a framework for the briefing. You now need to decide how exactly you are going to deliver it.

Activity 12

Some speakers prefer to write out their speech in full and then read it word for word. This is perhaps because they feel there is less risk of making a mistake. Note down one disadvantage of doing this.

_____

_____

If you just read out a full script:

■ it is likely to sound very artificial (it's difficult to write speech in a natural way);

■ your eyes will be focused on the paper most of the time (so you can't see the signals the people in the audience are sending you – such as smiles, nods of the head, and so on);

■ it will be difficult to establish 'rapport' – a two-way relationship – with the audience. When you have rapport you can keep the audience interested and carry them with you. And, equally, you can see what they are thinking and how well you are getting through to them. If necessary, you can adjust what you are saying.

So it is probably best to just keep your notes in front of you and use them simply to jog your memory from time to time. However, if you are going to use this approach, you need to be thoroughly familiar with what you are going to say – and that means practice.

So you need to practise your delivery and make sure than you know how long you will take, how fast to go, and what words to use.

Particularly if you are tackling an important briefing for the first time, it would be worth planning a really thorough programme of practice and rehearsal. You could plan it along the following lines:

	Step	**Action**
1	Private practice	Practise in private, using your notes, and practising any demonstrations you are going to include.
2	Record and play back	Record the whole briefing on audio cassette, then play it back to see how it sounds. Re-record it until you are happy with it.
3	Private audition	Ask colleagues, friends or family members to be the audience, and deliver the briefing to them; ask them what they think, how natural it sounded, whether it was too fast, too slow, too complicated, etc.
4	Dress rehearsal	Using your notes again, rehearse it fully, complete with visual aids and demonstrations.

And finally . . .

if you want to check that your own briefing is going to cover all the key elements needed for success ask yourself these five questions.

- Is it clear what the briefing is about?
- Is it clear who is involved?
- Is it clear why the subject of the briefing is important?
- Is it clear what is expected of the audience after the briefing?
- Is it clear how the audience can get further information?

A lot of work?

Perhaps, but it will be worth it!

Activity 13

In order to carry out this activity you will need to attend at least one briefing session or presentation given by someone else. If you are not normally invited to such events ask your manager to obtain permission for you to do so.

The aim is to observe and comment on how the person giving the briefing or presentation has planned and structured it. Watch and listen throughout the event and take notes.

Afterwards write a short description of how the speaker:

■ introduced the briefing or presentation and got started;
■ structured the subject matter to ensure that all important points were covered in the time available;
■ ensured that everyone had the opportunity to ask questions at appropriate points;
■ summed up at the end of the briefing.

Score the speaker out of ten for each of these four points, and explain briefly what the problems were, if any.

6 Conducting the briefing or presentation

Now let's look at what really matters to you – the briefing or presentation itself.

6.1 Getting the message across

First line manager, Raj, to team member, Cathy:

'Er, are you busy right now? What I mean is, is what you're doing really urgent … of course it is. I know it's all important … only these orders ought to go out tonight if possible. Could you try and fit them in? Perhaps when you've finished the others? OK, then. I'll leave it with you …'.

Activity 14 · 3 mins

What do you think the outcome of the above briefing will be?

_____

How effective do you think the briefing is?

_____

There may have been some kind of feedback confirming that the orders will be sent out tonight. Cathy might have smiled and nodded, or given the thumbs up. But on the face of it we don't know – and neither does Raj.

This is a very poor briefing:

■ Raj obviously wants the orders to 'go out tonight', but fails to give a clear instruction to that effect;
■ he clearly lacks assertiveness;
■ he seems to lack authority.

In practice this is a recipe for trouble. Raj may believe that he has made it clear that the orders are urgent; Cathy's understanding, however, is that it is up to her to decide. Tomorrow, if it turns out that the orders didn't go, there may be a row.

Activity 15 · 10 mins

Which of the following would be good techniques for making sure that your message gets across?

1	Repeat the central message at least once.
2	Speak loudly and clearly.
3	Keep it short and simple.
4	Be assertive rather than aggressive.
5	Use words and phrases that you are confident the team members will understand.
6	Check that they understand.
7	Use eye contact.

Numbers 1, 3, 5 and 6 are all excellent rules for effective communication. The others need some comment.

2	Speak loudly and clearly.

It is always better to speak clearly. Speaking loudly may be useful in a noisy environment, or when the audience is spread over a large area. However, in ordinary situations it may make you sound like a school teacher talking to a class of six-year-olds.

4	Be assertive rather than aggressive.

Assertiveness is usually good: it means making it clear what you want without being vague and without being aggressive. Aggressiveness always provokes a bad reaction and damages relations between people.

7	Use eye contact.

Make eye contact with as many people in the audience as possible, looking from one to another in turn as you speak. Stay focused on each one for a few seconds.

6.2 Speaking with confidence

To 'sell' an idea you have to 'sell' yourself.

You can't help but admire people who stand up confidently in front of a room of strangers and deliver a riveting and polished speech. It seems as though they must have been born with natural energy and confidence.

How come they are so good at it? How come they don't tremble and stutter with nerves? How do they manage to make everything they say seem so important and convincing?

It is tempting to think that they are a totally different kind of person from you – that they really are 'born public speakers'.

However, there is no such thing as a 'born public speaker'. Effective speaking is something of which we are all capable, but which we have to learn. It is simply not true that people who regularly speak in public have had that skill from birth.

So what makes them different? Only three things:

- they are determined to do it well;
- they have learned the necessary communication skills;
- they have practised a lot.

6.3 Dealing with nerves

Communicating with a group can be much harder than communicating with an individual because:

- the fact that there is an audience may put more pressure on you – especially if you are inclined to be nervous or self-conscious;
- it is a more complex task – there are more people to take account of;
- groups behave differently from the individuals who compose them – groups may take on a personality of their own.

All this means that you are under more pressure when dealing with a group, and may feel anxious. Anxiety is the body's automatic reaction to a situation in which it believes that it is facing a serious threat. People who are anxious show it in a number of physical ways.

Over a pint in the pub Jenny was telling her friends about the traumatic day she had been through at the call centre where she worked. She had been making a presentation to a group of visiting Japanese businessmen on the call-handling system used by her team.

'I was terrified. My head was sort of swimming, and somehow I couldn't see properly – everything was a blur. My heart was thumping away like mad. I started off in a great rush and gabbled like an idiot. My voice was all wobbly and I kept having to swallow because my throat was so dry.

'Then when I had settled down a bit I suddenly realised that my left leg was trembling uncontrollably, and I thought everyone must be able to see it. I lost my place, stuttered and started sweating all over. I don't really know how I got through to the end.

'When I'd finished I just wanted to run away and hide. I thought I'd be the laughing stock of the whole department. But the funny thing was that no one seemed to notice, and my manager actually said "Well done, Jenny – but take it a bit slower next time you do it." Next time! I couldn't go through that again.'

The reaction of fear or anxiety is natural in such a situation. But you can learn to deal with it by:

- learning to control your physical reactions;
- managing your thinking processes;
- improving your speaking techniques, and thus your self-confidence.

We have already had a quick look at speaking techniques, but it is worth spending a bit of time on the other two areas.

6.4 Controlling your physical reactions

Activity 16 · 3 mins

Think for a moment of somebody you have heard giving a speech, who you realized was nervous. Perhaps it was somebody at work, at a wedding or on television.

Jot down what signs the speaker gave that he or she was nervous.

_____

_____

> Relaxation techniques put the chemical flows created by anxiety into reverse, and are easy to learn. Many books are available on the subject.

Well, the ways of showing nervousness are endless. But common signs include:

■ blushing;
■ fiddling nervously with tie, cufflinks, jewellery, hair, papers;
■ frequent throat-clearing;
■ perspiring;
■ trembling hands;
■ voice too high-pitched, or not coming out at all.

Here are some simple hints for coping with the physical symptoms of anxiety:

■ give yourself time: walk a few metres to where you are going to speak;
■ spend a few seconds arranging your papers before you start;
■ clench your fists very tightly, and then relax them as slowly as you can, several times;
■ do breathing and voice control exercises;
■ learn relaxation techniques.

6.5 Managing your thinking processes

The problem with having a fear of speaking in front of other people is that it can become a self-fulfilling prophesy. If you think that something bad will happen, it will.

The best way to reduce your fear of speaking in public is to increase your confidence that you **can** do it competently.

Jeremy had worked for a utility company for ten years. He was the acknowledged expert on the company's electricity billing system, and if anyone had a problem, they naturally turned to Jeremy. So it seemed a great idea when the Director of Training and Development asked him to take on the training role in his section.

But then the panic set in. Jeremy had felt perfectly comfortable briefing his colleagues on a one to one basis. But the thought of standing up in front of eight or ten people and delivering a formal briefing filled him with dread. It reminded him of the time he had toasted the bridesmaids at his wedding – when he had forgotten what he was going to say, and had had to sit down to the cheers and laughter of the guests.

That bad experience had made Jeremy dread any form of speaking in public. He broke out in a sweat just thinking about it.

The good news is that, by learning to manage his thinking processes, Jeremy could change that memory from a nightmare into something positive.

Once you have experienced something it becomes a memory which is stored in your mind. When Jeremy reacted to the memory of his wedding, he was in fact reacting to the way the memory was stored in his mind – as a dark, threatening, terrifying ordeal. And it was this that was making him dread the future training sessions.

Good memories are usually remembered as bright, clear images, possibly in colour, perhaps a bit larger than life, associated with feelings of warmth and well-being. In contrast, bad memories may appear dull, colourless, indistinct and a bit distant.

Anne, one of Jeremy's colleagues, had just attended a course on neurolinguistic programming – the study of the relationship between thinking, language and behaviour, i.e. how people can learn to choose the ways they think, feel and behave. Anne explained, that, according to NLP, Jeremy could learn to 'manage' his memories so that they were stored in a way that resulted in his feeling the way he would like to feel.

With Anne's help, Jeremy learned to see his wedding speech as a warm, funny experience in which his friends were laughing **with**, rather than **at**, him.

When he eventually gave his first briefing, he felt the same warmth and good feeling that he – now – remembered having on his wedding day.

Activity 17

Think of a part of your work that you really enjoy. What do you see? What do you hear? What do you feel?

_____

_____

_____

Now think of a part of your work that you don't enjoy very much at all. In what way do you see, hear, feel it differently from the part you enjoy?

_____

_____

_____

If you can reprogramme your bad memory so that it is stored as a bright, 'good-feeling' memory, then it will give you strength and confidence to handle similar situations in the future.

6.6 The importance of feedback

Feedback is the information that the members of your team give you in response to your briefing. They do this all the time, whether you ask for it or not. If they are paying attention, by watching you and making eye contact when you look at them they are telling you that they are interested and listening to you. If they are playing with their pens, whispering to each other or gazing out of the window, the message is just as clear – we're not interested, we're bored, we don't care!

If the team members are interested and listening they will send other signals, such as nodding, making notes or by asking questions. These are all examples of **unprompted feedback** – feedback which you have not asked for but which you should be alert to. If you have a good relationship with your team they will want you to be successful at giving briefings, especially if you are nervous, and they will accentuate this feedback to let you know that you are being successful.

You can also ask for feedback by asking questions. Don't ask, 'Do you understand?' as this is too open and could leave you with the impression that people did understand simply because they weren't prepared to put their hand up and say, 'No!'. Why won't they? Because it may make them look silly, if they are alone, so people hope that someone else will explain it to them later. Unfortunately, if they all hope that, nobody can.

Instead you should ask specific questions:

■ Gill, will you be able to prepare the packets for dispatch if they arrive that late?
■ Paul, do you know how many days leave you are entitled to under this new system?
■ Petra, what do you think of the new schedule? Is it 'do-able'?

Feedback enables you to check that:

■ Your message has got through – people have heard it.
■ Any action will be taken – people understand it.
■ The purpose of your briefing has been achieved – that the team will go away and do what is needed.

7 When it's all over

After the briefing or presentation is over, you may well heave a sigh of relief and think you can forget all about it. No chance.

Activity 18

3 mins

What else do you think is left to be done?

_____

_____

There is no point in going through an experience like this if lessons aren't learnt from it.

■ Your manager and other relevant people need to be informed of any significant points that were raised during the briefing or presentation, and any action which should be taken as a result.

■ You need to carry out an evaluation (a kind of post mortem) to judge how well you did and what you could do better next time.

Let's look at each of these in a bit more detail.

7.1 Reporting back to management

As soon as the briefing or presentation is over you should make short notes of:

■ what you covered;
■ how the audience reacted;
■ any significant points raised and, if necessary, how you answered them;
■ any further action that needs to be taken.

You could send this in the form of a memo to your manager. Not only will it raise awareness of anything important that happened, but it will also remind your manager of your professional approach to the task you have been given.

7.2 Evaluating your performance

No one does a perfect briefing session or presentation first time round, because learning to speak effectively takes experience as well as preparation. As a beginner, you should be more than satisfied if you have been able to cover the content thoroughly in the time available.

But when you have a few competent performances under your belt, it is time to think about polishing up your act.

Activity 19

8 mins

Think back to the last few times you listened to someone giving a presentation or briefing. Think about how they delivered it, especially their behaviour. In what ways could they have improved their performance?

_____

_____

_____

_____

Some speakers are too technical, too quiet or too monotonous, but there can also be a problem caused by annoying habits and mannerisms. These irritate the audience and distract them from the speech itself. Here are some of the most common ones:

- irritating verbal mannerisms:

  - using catch phrases such as 'to be perfectly honest with you', or 'at the end of the day';
  - saying 'y'know', 'er' and 'well' every few words: 'Well, er, it's, well, got a very good, y'know, reputation for, er, quality. Well . . .';
  - clearing your throat nervously before each sentence;
  - muttering under your breath when changing a visual aid or doing a demonstration: 'OK, right . . . OHP slide on . . . right . . . there we are . . . right';

- irritating non-verbal mannerisms:

  - turning and talking to a flipchart instead of facing the audience;
  - facing the audience but never raising your eyes to look anyone in the face;
  - only looking at one person in the audience during the whole briefing;
  - continually walking back and forth in front of the audience;
  - fiddling constantly, for instance by clicking a pen cap on and off;
  - constantly moving your hands: waving around, in and out of your pockets, picking something up from the table, putting it down again, scratching your head, back in your pockets, up again to rub your nose.

There are many more bad habits like these – and they are almost all subconscious. People simply don't realize that they are doing them.

Activity 20

S/NVQ B6

This Activity may provide the basis of appropriate evidence for your S/NVQ portfolio. If you are intending to take this course of action, it might be better to write your answers on separate sheets of paper.

Think very hard about your own verbal and physical mannerisms when speaking in public. Ask people who have watched you talking in some formal situation or when the pressure has been on you for some other reason.

If possible, arrange for someone to video you, and watch the tape together afterwards.

Now write down your mannerisms, as honestly as you can. Note which were most likely to distract or irritate an audience.

_____

_____

_____

_____

_____

_____

_____

Now practise speaking without these mannerisms. It's usually best to tackle them one at a time, making sure you've eliminated each one before going on to the next.

Of course, an occasional gesture to emphasize a point is fine, but anything beyond that will get in the way of your message, making you less professional than you could be.

Finally, here is a very straightforward task for you: sit down and watch the television news.

- Watch the newsreaders carefully:
  - they are cool, calm, controlled and restrained;
  - they scarcely ever use a physical gesture, and they avoid irritating mannerisms.

- Listen to them carefully:
  - the words they use are always simple and straightforward;
  - they speak clearly and without hurrying;
  - they've learned to use small changes in the tone and pitch of their voice to fit the 'story', whatever it is.

Watch and listen carefully, because these are the professionals. Most people will never reach such dizzy heights, but it is always worth remembering that once they were just like everyone else. The only difference is that they have worked hard at it, practised their techniques and learned from long experience.

It is all a matter of learning the skills. They did it, and so can you.

8 Changing sides – being a contributor

As a first line manager you will inevitably be required to attend briefings and presentations given by other people.

When you attend a briefing or presentation, there are various reasons why you might be called upon to make a contribution. You might:

■ be responsible for providing further information on a topic in your specialist area;
■ ask questions;
■ provide answers to other people's questions.

So it is not enough just to turn up and leave all the work to the person giving the briefing or presentation.

As a member of the audience you share responsibility for the success of the event.

Activity 21

4 mins

What can the audience do to make sure a briefing or presentation goes well? Suggest two or three ideas.

_____

_____

_____

You could have said that the audience should:

■ listen attentively;
■ use encouraging body language;
■ ask relevant questions.

To put it simply, everyone who is being addressed should take a positive and constructive attitude and support the briefer's objective of trying to get through the briefing or presentation session in the time allowed with everything explained and understood.

A passive or hostile attitude, which often comes from people who 'hate briefings', certainly won't improve matters.

It also helps if the members of the audience:

- study any relevant documents beforehand;
- only ask questions at appropriate points in the briefing;
- keep any contributions short and to the point.

There are three reasons why you should try to make good quality contributions to a meeting:

- it will help the briefing or presentation to work better and produce better outcomes;
- you are more likely to achieve the outcomes you are personally seeking;
- it will improve your personal reputation and help your career.

Activity 22 · 3 mins

Write down six words that would describe a good quality contribution.

_____   _____

_____   _____

_____   _____

You probably listed words like 'relevant', 'coherent', 'brief', 'powerful', 'well-informed', 'well-argued', and so on. Actually the measure of quality is when listeners think to themselves 'That made a lot of sense', showing that the message got through and was both understandable and credible.

Self-assessment 1

20 mins

1 What is the hidden agenda that is part of all briefings and presentations?

_____

_____

2 I _____ and I forget.

I see and I _____.

I do and I _____.

3 When you are preparing to argue a case, you should find out the nature of any objections to it beforehand. Why?

_____

_____

4 What causes anxiety?

_____

_____

5 The structure of a briefing or presentation always consists of three distinct parts. What are they?

_____

_____

_____

6 Complete these sentences outlining three excellent reasons for using visual aids:

a Some things are easier to _____ visually than in speech.

b Visual aids help your listeners to _____ the points you are making.

c Visual aids make the whole presentation more _____ and _____.

7 What are the eight steps in carrying out a demonstration?

_____

_____

_____

_____

_____

_____

_____

_____

8 What four questions should you ask when selecting information to include in a briefing or presentation?

_____

_____

9 What do we mean when we say a speaker has 'rapport'?

_____

Answers to these questions can be found on pages 80–1.

9 Summary

- When you brief or give a presentation to your team:

    - you usually do so in order to achieve a particular objective;
    - but it always affects your working relationship with them.

- An effective briefing or presentation has outcomes that change the world in small but useful ways.

- A briefing or presentation is a two-way process in which your attention to feedback is crucial. It always pays to check that the messages have got through in the way you intended.

- For an effective briefing or presentation:

    - repeat the central message at least once;
    - speak clearly and assertively;
    - keep it short and simple;
    - use words and phrases that you are confident the team members will understand;
    - check that they do understand;
    - use visual aids to supplement your verbal messages;
    - speak calmly and at a gentle pace;
    - limit the amount of information you try to communicate.

- Planning a formal briefing should cover the following stages:

    - working out your objectives;
    - deciding the key points of the content;
    - working out a structure;
    - preparing appropriate visual aids and demonstrations;
    - practising and rehearsing.

- Using visual aids and demonstrations makes the briefing more interesting and the messages more memorable.

- In the briefing or presentation, your introduction, summary and conclusions are of major importance. You should plan them carefully.

- Body language plays a big role in communication. Make sure that it doesn't distract from or contradict your message.

- After the briefing or presentation is over you should make a report to your manager and carry out an evaluation of your performance.

- You should be prepared to contribute to briefings and presentations made by others and help make these a success.

Session B
Presenting information visually

1 Introduction

Visual presentation of information has more impact than someone standing up and talking, a block of text or long lists of numbers and is often easier to understand.

The techniques used here are particularly useful when preparing visual aids for an oral briefing, but they also apply to written briefings and reports.

This final session, therefore, contains a range of advice about the most common methods of visual presentation of data used in business.

You don't have to be a talented artist: everything we describe here can be done using a word processor, a spreadsheet or other sources close to hand.

2 Tables

Tables present data in rows and columns. This form of presentation makes it easier to understand large amounts of data. A railway timetable is a familiar example.

Charing Cross	15:38	16:08	16:18	16:28	16:37	16:45	16:58
Waterloo	15:41	16:11	16:21	16:31	16:40	16:48	17:01
London Bridge	15:49	16:19	16:29	16:39	16:48	16:56	17:09
New Cross	16:01	16:31	16:41	—	17:00	17:08	17:21
Lewisham	16:06	16:36	16:46	16:50	17:05	17:13	17:26

Activity 23

3 mins

You arrive at London Bridge at 16:42 and you want to go to Lewisham. Note down at least three things that this timetable tells you.

There are lots of possible answers: this activity was intended to make you think about the various ways you can use tables. Here are some possibilities.

- You can look up a specific value by seeing where rows and columns meet. Since you know it is 16:42 you can quickly see from the timetable that your next train is due in six minutes (at 16:48) and will arrive in Lewisham at 17:05.
- You can work your way around the table from your original starting point and test out other scenarios. For instance, you can see that if you had arrived at London Bridge a few minutes earlier you could have got a fast train. If you are not sure that six minutes is long enough to buy a cup of coffee and a bar of chocolate you can get a slightly later train to Lewisham which will give you 14 minutes.
- You can read across rows (or down columns) and compare values. For future reference you can note (by reading right across the London Bridge row) that from 16:19 onwards there is a train to Lewisham roughly every ten minutes.

Tables are a simple way of presenting numerical information. Figures are displayed, and can be compared with each other: relevant totals, subtotals and percentages can also be presented as a summary for analysis.

A table is two-dimensional (rows and columns): so it can only show two variables: a sales analysis for a year, for example, might have rows for months, and columns for products.

SALES FIGURES FOR 2004

	Product A	Product B	Product C	Product D	Total
Jan	370	651	782	899	2,702
Feb	718	312	748	594	2,372
Mar	548	204	585	200	1,537
Apr	382	616	276	359	1,633
May	132	241	184	223	780
Jun	381	216	321	123	1,041
Jul	679	612	733	592	2,616
Aug	116	631	343	271	1,361
Sep	421	661	868	428	2,378
Oct	211	158	653	479	1,501
Nov	306	243	676	404	1,629
Dec	898	759	796	394	2,847
Total	5,162	5,304	6,965	4,966	22,397

You are likely to present data in tabular form very often. Here are the key points to remember.

- The table should have a clear title.
- All columns and rows should be clearly labelled.
- Where appropriate, there should be sub-totals and a right-hand total column for comparison.
- A total figure is often advisable at the bottom of each column of figures also, for comparison. It is usual to double-underline totals at the foot of columns where the table is not presented in a grid.
- Numbers should be right-aligned and they are easier to read if you use the comma separator for thousands.
- Decimal points should line up, either by using a decimal tab or by adding extra zeros (the latter is preferable, in our opinion).

Wrong (Left aligned)	Wrong (Right aligned)	Right (OK)	Right (Best)
12.5	12.5	12.5	12.50
13.64	13.64	13.64	13.64
2.9	2.9	2.9	2.90
135	135	135.0	135.00

- A grid or border is optional: see what looks best and is easiest to read (in the above example we've used a grid to illustrate the alignment of numbers more clearly).
- Tables should not be packed with too much data; if you try to get too much in, the information presented will be difficult to read.

2.1 Columns or rows?

Often it will be obvious which information should go in the columns and which should go in rows. Sometimes, it won't matter too much which way round you have the rows and columns. Here are some points to remember.

It is usually easier to read across a short line than a long one. That means that it is usually better to have a long thin table than a short wide one: lots of rows rather than lots of columns. If you had a price list of five hundred products each of which came in three different sizes, you would probably tabulate the information like this, without even considering the other possibility (it wouldn't fit on the paper or screen, anyway, if you had products in columns).

Product	Large	Medium	Small
A001	12.95	11.65	9.35
A002	14.50	12.50	10.50
A003	etc.	etc.	etc.
A004			
A005			
etc.			

However, most people find it easier to compare figures by reading across than by reading down. For example in the previous version of the sales figures it is easier to compare product totals, but in the version below it is easier to compare monthly totals.

	Jan	Feb	Mar	Apr	May	Jun	Jul	Aug	Sep	Oct	Nov	Dec	Total
Product A	370	718	548	382	132	381	679	116	421	211	306	898	5,162
Product B	651	312	204	616	241	216	612	631	661	158	243	759	5,304
Product C	782	748	585	276	184	321	733	343	868	653	676	796	6,965
Product D	899	594	200	359	223	123	592	271	428	479	404	394	4,966
Total	2,702	2,372	1,537	1,633	780	1,041	2,616	1,361	2,378	1,501	1,629	2,847	22,397

If you are not sure what your readers will most want to compare it might be helpful to give them both versions, if practicable.

The table shown here is quite large, with fourteen columns in all. This is okay for a written document but would not work well in a presentation as a visual aid. It would have to have quite small figures to fit and would be hard to read at a distance. If you wanted to show this to a group, then you would be better to give everyone a copy to look at close up.

3 Line graphs

In business, line graphs are usually used to illustrate trends over time of figures such as sales or customer complaints (what is known as a 'time series').

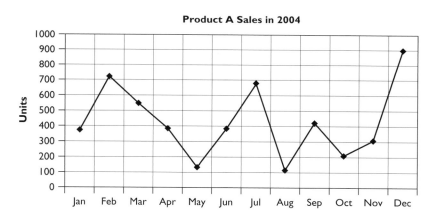

The figures are plotted on a grid and then joined by a line that reflects the 'ups and downs' of the figure, over a period of time. Note that it is conventional to show **time** on the **horizontal axis.**

Now the trend in sales is shown instantly, in a way that is probably not immediately apparent from a column or row of figures. This encourages us to ask questions: for instance why did sales drop in the early months of the year and suddenly shoot up in June and July?

By using different symbols for the plotted points, or preferably by using different colours, several lines can be drawn on a line graph before it gets too overcrowded, and that means that several trends (for example the sales performance of different products) can be compared.

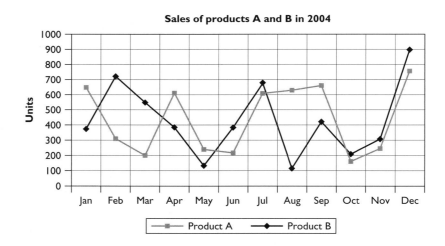

The scale of the vertical axis should be just large enough for you to tell with reasonable accuracy the sales figure at any given point during the period. In the example above we have used a scale of 100 and you can tell, for instance, that sales of product A in April were a little less than 400 (check in the table given in part 2 of this session).

Activity 24

Looking at the graph, what do products A and B have in common?

_____

_____

_____

_____

The answer to this Activity is on page 82.

4 Charts

We'll run through an extended exercise on creating charts without having to get your ruler and crayons out in the next part of this session, but first we'll make some comments in general about the types of chart you are likely to use most often in business reports: bar charts and pie charts.

4.1 Bar charts

The bar chart is one of the most common methods of visual presentation. Data is shown in the form of bars which are the same in width but variable in height. Each bar represents a different item, for example the annual production cost of different products or the number of hours required to produce a product by different workteams.

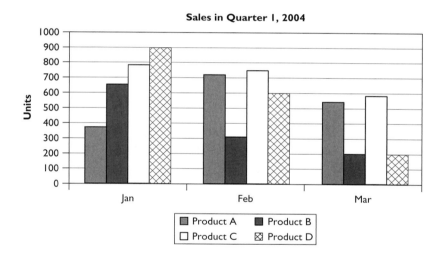

As you can see, here we are more interested in comparing a few individual items in a few individual months (although you can still get a visual impression of trends over time).

Activity 25

2 mins

Comment on sales of products A and B, based on the chart above.

_____

_____

_____

_____

Our answer to this Activity is on page 82.

Horizontal presentation is also possible.

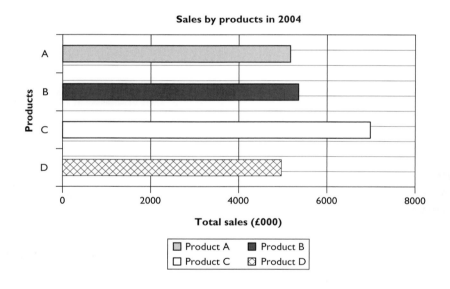

Sales by products in 2004

There are no hard and fast rules about whether you should use vertical or horizontal presentation. However, these guidelines may help.

- If you are showing trends over time (for instance January to March) vertical bars look best.
- If you are showing differences at a single point in time (the end of 2004, for instance) you might prefer horizontal bars.

4.2 Pie charts

A pie chart shows the relative sizes of the things that make up a total. It is called a pie chart because it is shaped like a pie and is cut into 'slices'.

Pie charts are most effective where the number of slices is small enough to keep the chart simple, and where the difference in the size of the slices is large enough for the eye to judge without too much extra information.

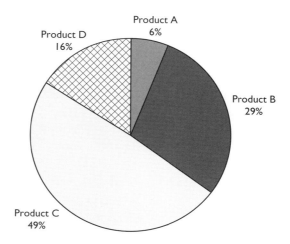

5 How to create charts in Excel

Microsoft Excel has a superb tool for creating hundreds of different charts, graphs and diagrams. We cannot cover all the options in this book, but we will work through the basics for one type of chart. You should then have enough knowledge to be able to experiment on your own.

As we'll see in a moment, the easiest way to create a chart in Excel is to select your data and press F11. However, unless you understand the basics of the Excel Chart Wizard this can often produce unexpected or unwanted results.

Activity 26 ·

The whole of this section on charts and Excel is really an extended Activity based on the initial data below.

Create a new folder on your computer with a name such as Briefing_and_Presentation_Skills. Open Excel and save the new workbook with a name such as 'YourName_PerfectTen.xls' in this folder.

PERFECT TEN MODEL AGENCY

Perfect Ten is a model agency. Currently it handles the careers of 5 models: Ms White, Ms Red, Ms Green, Ms Yellow and Ms Blue.

Each model is rated each month on a scale of 1 to 10.

Here are the ratings for January to March. You should enter this data in cells A1 to F4 of your spreadsheet and then save your work.

	White	Red	Green	Yellow	Blue
January	10	9	7	8	6
February	10	5	7	3	4
March	10	7	3	2	1

We are going to work on this data to produce a variety of bar charts.

5.1 F11

The quickest way to create a chart in Excel is to use the F11 function key at the top of your keyboard.

- Select cells A1 to F4.
- Press F11.

This will create a chart in a separate spreadsheet called Chart 1.

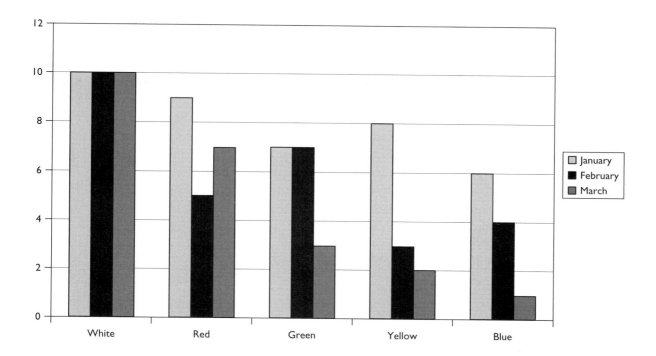

This is quick and easy, but the chances are that this is not how you wanted the chart to look.

To get a bit more control you need to use the Chart Wizard.

5.2 The Chart Wizard

The second quickest way to create a chart in Excel is to use the Chart Wizard. He lives in a little button near the top of the screen.

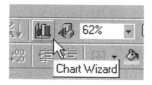

Activity 27

Create a clustered column chart with the model agency data by following these steps.

1   Select cells A1 to F4 again and click on the **Chart Wizard** button. This takes you to 'Step 1' of a four-step process.

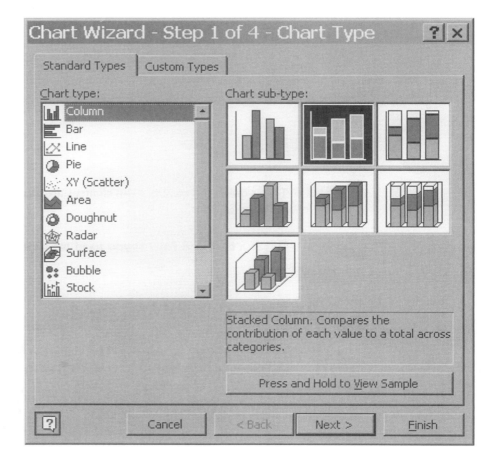

There are all sorts of options here and we will look at several of them, but now we are going to create a column chart of the first sub-type, clustered column.

2   Click on **Next** to go to Step 2.

3   Click **Next** on Step 2 and on Step 3 without making any changes. When you get to step 4 you will see the following options.

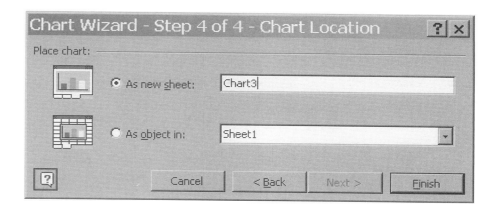

4   We don't want a new sheet this time, so make sure that the chart location is 'As object in Sheet 1' then click on Finish. Your chart will appear on the same page as your data.

Don't forget to save your spreadsheet.

5.3 RelaX!

Your chart should look like this.

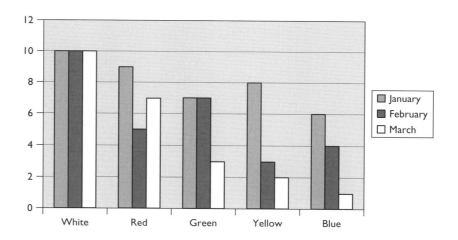

Let's pause to think about how the data has been presented in the charts.

First we need to learn a bit of terminology.

- The little square box on the right-hand side, containing the words January, February, March, is called the **legend**.
- The **horizontal** line, labelled White, Red, etc., is called the **X axis**.
- The **vertical** line, labelled with numbers 0, 2, 4, etc., is called the **Y axis**.

If you find it hard to remember which axis is which just think of the word **relaX**. The X-axis is the one that is having a lie down: in other words X is the horizontal one!

Excel also uses some other names: the X axis is called the **category** axis, and the Y axis is called the **value** axis.

5.4 What goes where?

Here's the data, with the chart underneath.

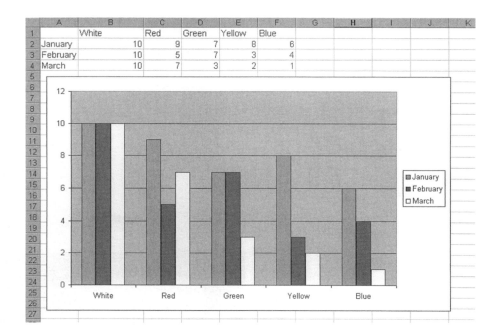

Activity 28

How do the three elements (legend, X axis, Y axis) relate to the original data?

_____

_____

_____

- The **legend** is derived from the **row labels**.
- The **X axis** is derived from the **column headings**.
- The **Y axis** is derived from the minimum and maximum **numbers** in the body of the table of data.

In fact the default behaviour in Excel is to derive the **X axis** from whatever there is more of, whether they are columns or rows. In this case we have more models than months, so the models go in the X axis. However, you don't have to accept this.

5.5 Changing what goes where

Here's the data and the chart once again.

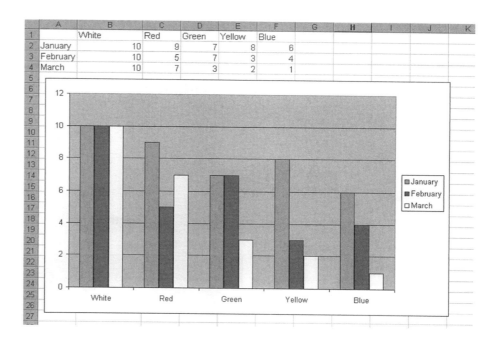

Suppose we wanted the X axis to show the months and the legend to show the girls' names? Do we have to change our original table of data?

The answer is no, of course. Here's how you do it.

1 Right click on a white area of the chart. A menu appears, from which you can choose **Source data**. You will see the following options.

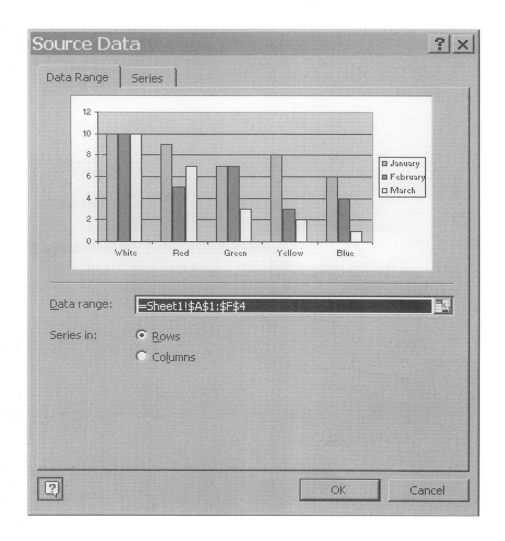

2   The **series** is just another word for what appears in the **legend** box. Select **Columns** and you will immediately see (in the preview shown in your Source data window) that this has done exactly what you wanted: the X axis shows the months; the girls' names (the **column headings**) are in the legend.

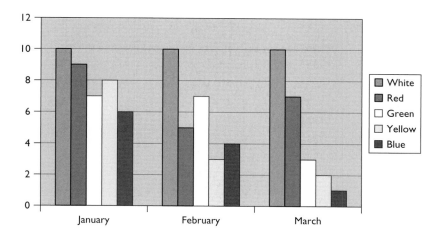

Activity 29

5 mins

Although there isn't space to go into the details, you can do a lot of editing and formatting of your chart after you've created it, simply by right-clicking on it and choosing from the options.

For instance, the bars representing the models will have come out in default colours chosen by Excel, but you can easily change this: right-click on any of the bars representing Ms White, say, and choose **Format data** series from the menu that appears. This gives you the opportunity to change the colour to something more appropriate: white, say.

Try this, and then see what other changes you can make to improve the appearance of your chart.

5.6 Changing the data

Some more information has come in and you need to revise some of your data.

In January, Ms Blue changed her name to Navy.

After reappraisal it has been decided that Ms Navy should have scored 4 in March. And although it is quite unprecedented Ms White scored 11 in February.

	A	B	C	D	E	F
1		White	Red	Green	Yellow	Navy
2	January	10	9	7	8	6
3	February	11	5	7	3	4
4	March	10	7	3	2	4

Activity 30

Make the above changes to your original data and watch the effect on the chart. It will update automatically.

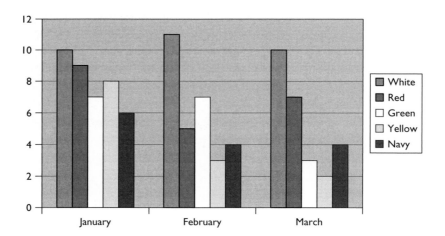

5.7 Other styles of bar charts

You can produce several other types of chart. The instructions below are for a 100% stacked chart on a new sheet within the workbook, using the data we have already created.

1 Select **Sheet 2** and **re-enter the original data**, without any of the changes you've made so far (you could just copy and paste from Sheet 1 and then change the data back to the original values).

2 Highlight cells A1 to F4 and click on the **Chart Wizard** button.

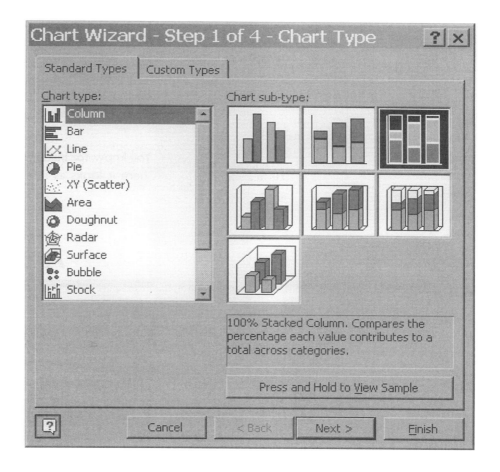

3 Select the **Column** chart type and the **Chart** sub-type, **100% Stacked**, as shown above.

4 Click on **Next** to go to Step 2 of the Wizard. Select the **Series in columns** option.

5 Click on **Next**.

6 At Step 3, Click on **Next** without making any changes.

7 At Step 4 click on **Finish** without making any changes.

The new chart would look like this.

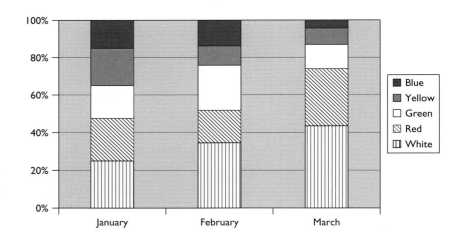

This is all very peculiar. You know, for instance, that Ms White scored a perfect 10 in each month, but here it looks as if her score is getting higher, month after month.

Activity 31

2 mins

Can you explain why it looks as if Ms White's score is getting higher each month?

_____

_____

_____

To make sense of this take a look again at the data.

	A	B	C	D	E	F
1		White	Red	Green	Yellow	Blue
2	January	10	9	7	8	6
3	February	10	5	7	3	4
4	March	10	7	3	2	1

Ms White does indeed score consistently, but the others don't. Most of their scores are getting lower and lower as time goes by. That means that Ms White's score as a percentage of the overall team score gets higher, month by month.

Prove this to yourself. Select cells G2 to G4 and then click on the **AutoSum** button at the top of the page.

Now you can see that Ms White contributed only 25% (10/40) to the overall team score in January, but almost 50% (10/23) in March. And that is exactly what is shown in the chart.

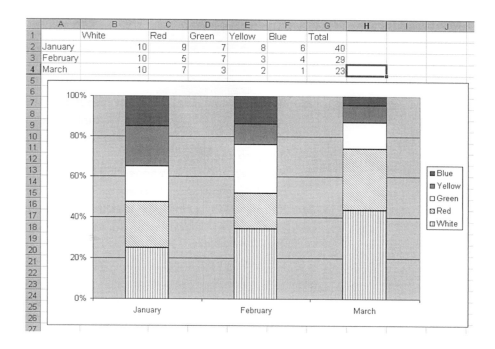

You should now know enough to experiment with charts using some real data of your own. Have a go at creating line graphs and pie charts as well as bar charts.

6 Other types of visual presentation

6.1 Flow charts, organization charts and other labelled diagrams

Flow charts and organization charts are useful ways of presenting and summarizing information that involves a series of steps and choices and/or relationships between the different items.

On the following pages there are some examples of this type of presentation.

If you choose any of these forms of presentation here are some points to bear in mind.

- Be consistent in your use of layout and symbols (and colours, if used). For instance, in our flow chart example a decision symbol is always a diamond with italic text; a YES decision always flows downwards; a NO decision always flows to the right.
- Keep the number of connecting lines to a minimum and avoid lines that 'jump over' each other at all costs.
- Keep the labels or other text brief and simple.
- Hand-drawn diagrams should be as neat and legible as possible. If they are likely to be seen by a lot of people (not just your team) it is better to use a business graphics programme like Microsoft Visio.
- Everyone can draw, but only so well. If you are not expert you can waste an enormous amount of time playing with computer graphics. If it needs to be really beautifully presented and you are not an expert sketch it quickly by hand and then give it to a professional.

A flowchart

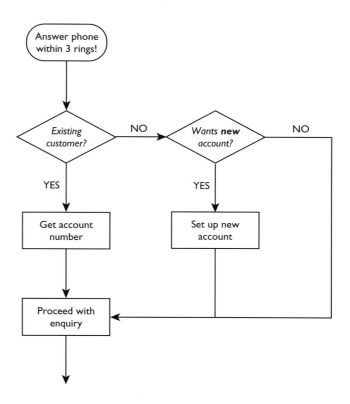

An organization chart

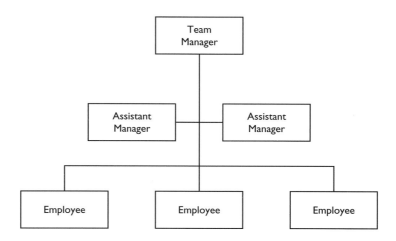

A key point summary

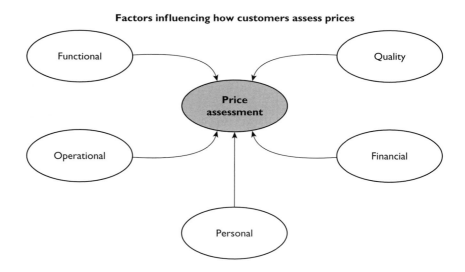

Factors influencing how customers assess prices

Activity 32 · 30 mins

Look at our examples and then create the following charts for your own workteam.

■ An organization chart.
■ A flow chart setting out how to do a work procedure that everybody on your team does regularly.

6.2 Pictograms

A pictogram is a simple graphic image in which the data is represented by a picture or symbol, with a clear key to the items and quantities intended. Different pictures can be used on the same pictogram to represent different elements of the data. For example, a pictogram showing the number of people employed by an organization might use pictures of . . . people.

Employees in 2003

Employees in 2004

100 male employees

100 female employees

You can see quite easily that the workforce has grown and that the organization employs far more female workers than before.

Pictograms present data in a simple and appealing way. They are often used on television. Watch out for them next time you are watching a news item involving numbers (number of trains late, number of new jobs created, and so on). In pictograms:

- the symbols must be clear and simple;
- there should be a key showing the number that each symbol represents;
- bigger quantities are shown by more symbols, not bigger symbols.

Bear in mind, however, that pictograms are not appropriate if you need to give precise figures. You can use portions of a symbol to represent smaller quantities, but there are limits to what you can do.

150 female employees

Over 100 employees, mostly male. But how many others and what sex are they?

6.3 Drawings and graphics

A labelled drawing may sometimes be the best way of presenting a lot of information in a small space. Imagine how difficult it would be to explain all the information you get from the following diagram if you could only use words!

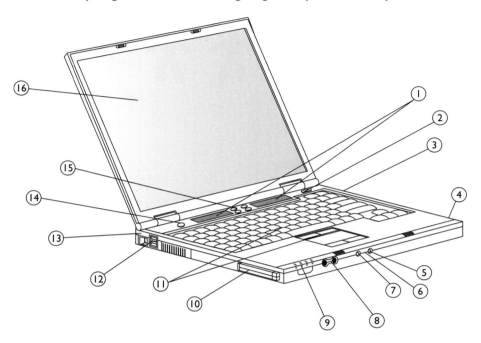

1. Stereo Speakers	9. System LEDs
2. Power Switch	10. PC Card Slots (2)
3. RJ-11 (Modem)	11. Touchpad + Pointstick
4. Cable Lock Connector	12. USB (2)
5. Audio-In	13. Keyboard LEDs
6. Microphone	14. Suspend Button
7. Headphone-out	15. Easy access Internet Button
8. Volume Controls	16. Colour Display

Activity 33 · 10 mins

Where might you obtain pictures and graphics such as the pictogram or the computer diagram shown above?

_____

_____

_____

_____

The answer to this Activity is on page 82.

6.4 Maps

Maps can be used to present information which is geographically-based, for example different sales areas.

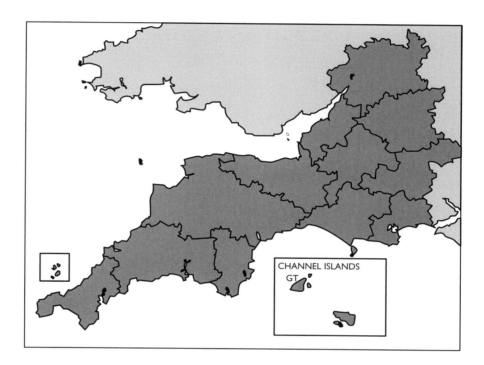

Local road maps or detailed street maps are often sent out to customers who may wish to visit the company's branches, or to people attending a meeting.

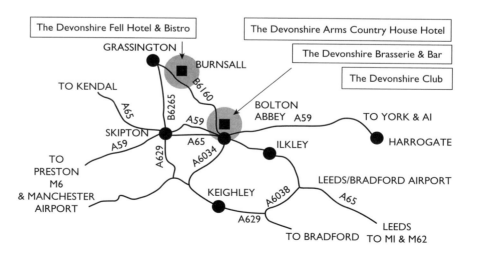

Self-assessment 2

10 mins

1 Fill in the missing words using words from this list.

long, right; short; thin; wide.

Numbers in a table should be _____ -aligned. It is usually better to have a _____ _____ table than a _____ _____ table.

2 Create a line graph (either by hand or by using a spreadsheet) based on the following information.

Units	Production cost
0	0
10	1,000
20	1,400
30	1,450
40	1,475
50	2,600

■ What does your graph show you?

_____

_____

_____

■ A pie chart would be a better way of showing this data. True/False.

3 When you create a chart using Excel the horizontal axis (also known as the X/Y* axis or category/value/series* axis) is derived from:

■ row labels
■ column headings
■ either rows or column headings

depending on the situation*.

(*Delete as applicable.)

Answers to these questions can be found on page 81.

7 Summary

- Tables are a simple way of presenting numerical and/or textual information. Figures are displayed, and can be compared with each other: relevant totals, subtotals, percentages can also be presented as a summary for analysis. Clear labels and headings and proper alignment are issues to consider.

- Line graphs are usually used to illustrate trends over time of figures such as sales. It is conventional to show time on the horizontal axis. Line graphs can help draw attention to questions that need to be asked and (within limits) can be used to compare performance.

- In a bar chart, data is shown in the form of vertical or horizontal bars which are the same in width but variable in height. Each bar represents a different item, so bar charts are generally more useful than graphs for comparisons.

- A pie chart is useful if you want to show the relative sizes of the things that make up a total.

- A large variety of charts and diagrams can be generated by the charting tools in spreadsheet programs such as Microsoft Excel.

- Other types of visual presentation used in business include organization charts, flow charts, pictograms, drawings or other graphics and maps.

Performance checks

1 Quick quiz

Question 1   What is the main purpose of a briefing?

_____

_____

Question 2   What three rules should you remember when briefing people you don't know much about?

_____

_____

_____

Question 3   What five steps are involved in planning and preparing a briefing?

_____

_____

_____

_____

_____

Question 4   Which part of the briefing should you design first?

_____

Question 5   Before you begin your briefing, you should check that:

■ all your _____ _____ are ready;

■ the _____ is set up and working properly.

Question 6   Suggest four techniques for making sure that your message gets across to your audience.

_____

_____

_____

_____

Question 7   What three pieces of information does feedback give the original sender of a message?

_____

_____

_____

Question 8   The manually produced bar chart below has been incorrectly drawn. What is wrong with it?

_____

_____

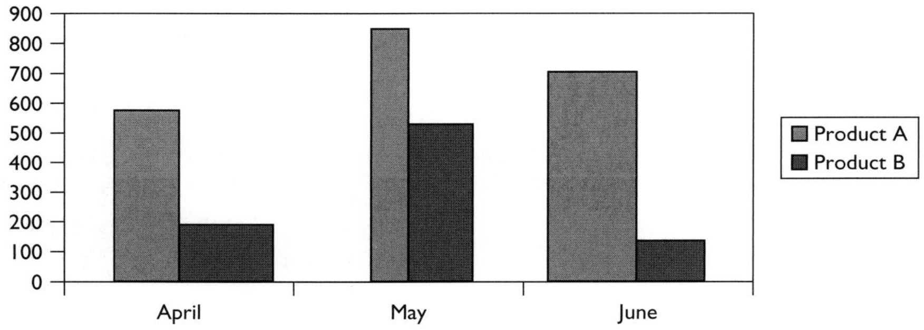

Question 9   How can you edit and/or format an Excel chart after you have created it?

_____

_____

Question 10   Give one advantage and one disadvantage of a pictogram.

_____

_____

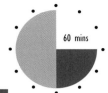

 # 2 Workbook assessment

Read the following case incident and then deal with the questions which follow, writing your answers on a separate sheet of paper.

Angelica Kiprianou has just taken over as day-shift team leader in the technical support department of a large insurance company. The department's role is to solve computer and telecommunications problems for staff in other departments. Since much of the company's business is done by telephone, fax and e-mail, and virtually everyone uses computers, this is a crucial role. The workload is heavy and the pressures are intense.

Angelica's predecessor, Keith Roberts, was a notorious 'hard man' who supervised everyone extremely strictly. His objectives for his team were simple: repair faults quickly, but avoid if at all possible replacing faulty equipment with new. Any complaint about slowness in carrying out a repair made him furious; he was equally angry if a technician decided to replace a unit instead of repairing it. Roberts, who was a big man, would stomp into the repair shop and shout abuse at the culprit in front of the whole department. This aside, though, he was uncommunicative. The team had little idea of what the company as a whole was doing, or of how their own work fitted into the broader picture.

Angelica is quite different – she is a competent team leader while being pleasant and quietly spoken. She does not want to run the department in the way that Roberts did – and probably couldn't even if she wanted to.

After a few weeks, Angelica notices that costs are increasing and that faulty equipment is piling up. She soon realizes that the technicians are taking advantage of her by replacing equipment with new units instead of repairing the faults. This suits both the customers and the technicians. However, it is very wasteful, and Angelica will in due course be accountable for the rising cost of new equipment.

She also notes that technicians are tending to dump replaced equipment in the store room without any indication of what the fault was. This will cause much confusion and extra work when someone finally sits down to repair these units; and, naturally enough, the backlog of repairs is steadily growing.

Angelica needs to restore the working practices that Roberts had established, but in her own way.

She decides to have a team briefing.

Carry out the following tasks:

1 Make a list of the key points and subsidiary points that Angelica would include in the briefing, then write brief notes for an introduction, summary and conclusion.

2 What data could Angelica use to emphasize the problems she is addressing in her briefing? How could she best present this data to make her point clearly?

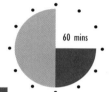

3 Work-based assignment

S/NVQ
B6

The time guide for this assignment gives you an idea of how long it is likely to take you to write up your findings. You will find that you need to spend some additional time gathering information, perhaps talking to colleagues and thinking about the assignment. The result of your efforts should be presented as speaking notes and draft visual aids, plus a recording on audio or video cassette.

Your written response to this assignment may form useful evidence for your S/NVQ portfolio. The assignment is designed to help you demonstrate your skills in:

■ briefing others.

What you should do

Prepare a briefing session about how the work of your team is organized, supervised and evaluated, i.e. how you carry out your personal role as manager or team leader. The audience is a visiting delegation from Germany. The members of the delegation all speak good, but not perfect English, and you will need to make allowances for this.

The briefing should not take more than 10 minutes in its final form.

Make neat drafts of three flip-chart pages or three OHP or PowerPoint slides which you would propose to use as visual aids.

- Prepare a neat copy of the notes from which you would speak.
- Practise and rehearse delivering the briefing, perhaps with the help of friends.
- When you are happy with it, make an audio or video recording of the presentation (depending on what facilities you have available).

Remember that your presentation should cover all the key points while not taking more than 10 minutes to deliver.

Reflect and review

▪ 1 Reflect and review

Now that you have completed your work on *Giving Briefings and Making Presentations in the Workplace* let's review the workbook objectives. The first objective was:

■ prepare and deliver effective briefings to your team, and contribute to briefings given by others.

On completion of this workbook you will be better able to ensure that when you give a briefing, your listeners will understand you clearly.

Thinking about the audience is the key to successful briefings, whether it is on a one-to-one basis or in front of a group.

Listeners are all different, and you cannot always assume that they understand the jargon of your workplace or share your understanding of the subject. People misunderstand each other easily enough in ordinary life; at work it pays for managers and team leaders to make certain that their messages are getting through. There are two main points to remember:

■ some listeners may need more explanation than others;
■ you need to check their understanding.

Think about the range of people you have to brief, and the different things you need to say to them.

■ Who needs more explanation?

_____

_____

■ How will you check understanding?

_____

_____

■ How can you improve your presentation skills?

_____

_____

_____

The other objectives concerned the presentation of information.

■ Select the most appropriate way to present statistical information.
■ Present charts and diagrams effectively.
■ Interpret statistical information from tables, charts or diagrams.

Sometimes it is enough to present the information in a simple table, as long as you remember all the rules about headings and alignment and totals. Charts and diagrams can be very useful ways of summarizing information and showing up trends that may not be apparent if all you have is a mass of figures. The most commonly used types in business are graphs, bar charts and pie charts.

The best way to create a business chart is to use a spreadsheet charting tool. This is very easy in theory but needs a little practice to get the data exactly as you want it. That raises another issue: you should of course be able to explain in words what your charts mean.

■ Get into the habit of summarizing your data in the form of charts and graphs. You may not always use the charts you create in your final report but they are quick and easy to create if you use the right tools and they may draw attention to trends that would otherwise go unnoticed.

Make a note of any charts that you could produce regularly to illustrate your team's current performance and performance targets.

_____

_____

_____

_____

2 Action plan

Use this plan to further develop for yourself a course of action you want to take. Make a note in the left-hand column of the issues or problems you want to tackle, and then decide what you intend to do, and make a note in column 2.

The resources you need might include time, materials, information or money. You may need to negotiate for some of them, but they could be something easily acquired, like half an hour of somebody's time, or a chapter of a book. Put whatever you need in column 3. No plan means anything without a timescale, so put a realistic target completion date in column 4.

Finally, describe the outcome you want to achieve as a result of this plan, whether it is for your own benefit or advancement, or a more efficient way of doing things.

Desired outcomes			
1 Issues	2 Action	3 Resources	4 Target completion
Actual outcomes			

3 Extensions

Extension 1   *Using visual aids*

The **overhead projector** (OHP) is one of the simplest and most effective visual aids. It is particularly valuable for keeping important points in front of you listeners while your are talking about them. OHPs are useful for diagrams, cartoons and other illustrations, as well as text.

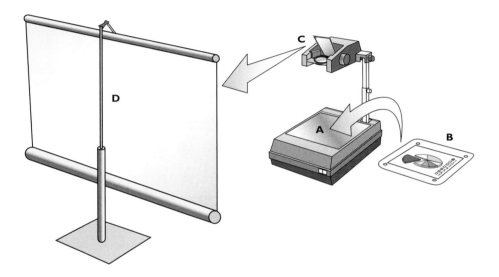

It is basically a box with a back-lit opaque panel on the top (A). You place your slide (B) on top of this panel, and the lens (C) picks up the image and casts it onto a screen (D). This creates a greatly enlarged image, big enough for the audience to read.

Making OHP slides is very easy. The slides themselves are made of heat-resistant plastic film, and all you need to write on them is one or two special felt-tip pens in different colours. The techniques for successful OHP slides are:

OHP slides can also be prepared on a computer and printed out through a laser or ink-jet printer. You can add colour by hand if necessary.

■   write or draw clearly;
■   write or draw neatly;
■   don't try to cram on too much information.

In fact it is most important to draft out your OHP sheet on plain paper, to make sure you have got it right before you put pen to plastic!

Here are two examples of OHP slides, both much reduced from the normal size of about 20 cm × 30 cm:

Bad   **Good**

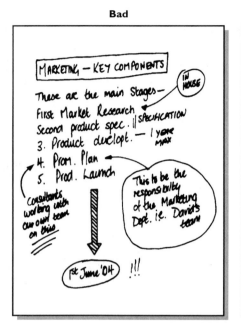 

When you are talking about what the slide shows, you can point to particular parts of it, and there are techniques for this too:

- use a pencil or a pointer and point to the slide itself, not the screen (the lens will project the pointer onto the screen);
- keep facing the audience, and don't be tempted to turn round and look at the screen while you are talking (this is bad body language and also makes you hard to hear).

Computer-based projectors are increasingly replacing OHPs for use in making presentations. Projectors need to be connected to a computer and then projected on to a screen. The presentations need to be prepared using appropriate software. The most widely used is Microsoft's PowerPoint™ programme.

The image shows a **template** for the ILM's PowerPoint™ presentations. Templates are a standard presentation layout that allow you to enter your own words and images. Many organizations have templates for their organization's presentations. If your organization doesn't have its own template, there are many standard templates with the software that you can choose from.

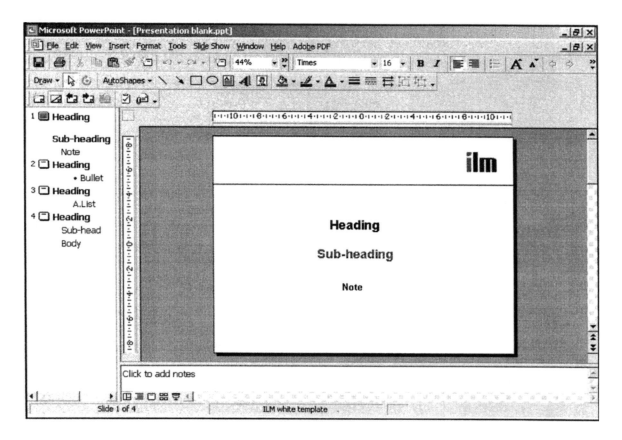

Some points about using computer-based presentations:

■ Avoid making a presentation too fussy. Use simple text and graphic formats and aim for simplicity. Learn what works and what doesn't before you use every possible capability of the system.

■ Keep font sizes large, around 18 point minimum. It's possible for text to appear in different ways, moving in from the sides, bouncing, swivelling, forming from a checkerboard, etc. Don't use more than one such effect on each slide, and use the same one for each slide. If you don't you will find that the audience is paying more attention to the effects than the words.

■ You have a huge choice of colours (and images), but you should use only two or three unless it's absolutely necessary to use more. Make them strong colours as well, avoiding pale colours that may not show up clearly.

■ With digital cameras so widely available, you can add high quality still pictures and even audio and video recordings as part of a presentation, so why describe something you can show?

4 Answers to self-assessment questions

Self-assessment 1 on pages 33–4

1 The hidden agenda is the feelings and attitudes that affect working relationships.

2 I **HEAR** and I forget.
I see and I **REMEMBER**.
I do and I **UNDERSTAND**.

3 If you know the nature of any objections to what you are going to say you will avoid being 'ambushed' and can deal with them in your own contribution.

4 Anxiety is the body's automatic reaction to a situation in which it believes that it is facing a serious threat.

5 A briefing or presentation should consist of:

■ an introduction
■ a main part
■ a summary and conclusion

6 a Some things are easier to **COMMUNICATE** visually than in speech.
  b Visual aids help your listeners to **REMEMBER** the points you are making.
  c Visual aids make the whole presentation more **INTERESTING** and **CREDIBLE**.

7 The eight steps in carrying out a demonstration are:

1	Introduce the subject and describe what is required.
2	Explain why.
3	Explain when the new procedure is to be used.
4	Demonstrate how to carry out the procedure.
5	Ask team members to do it for themselves.
6	Correct and advise them where necessary.
7	Check understanding and competence.
8	If necessary, repeat steps 4 to 7.

8   The four questions to ask yourself are:

- what sort of people are in my audience?
- what are the **key** facts and feelings I want to pass on to them, i.e. what are my objectives?
- what do they know already?
- what are their current attitudes and feelings?

9   Rapport is a good two-way relationship between the speaker and the audience.

Self-assessment 2 on page 64

1   Numbers in a table should be **RIGHT**-aligned. It is usually better to have a **LONG THIN** table than a **SHORT WIDE** table.

2   This is our graph, produced with Microsoft Excel:

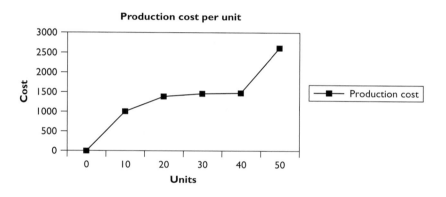

Production cost per unit

The graph clearly shows that production costs per unit gradually fall up to the level of 40 units, but then rise dramatically if more than 40 units are produced. This would probably be because one person or one machine could produce no more than 40 units: if you wanted 50 you would have to get a second person or machine.

A pie chart would be quite unsuitable for this sort of data. A bar chart would show it equally well, however.

3   When you create a chart using Excel the horizontal axis (also known as the **X** axis or **CATEGORY** axis) is derived from: **EITHER ROW LABELS OR COLUMN HEADINGS, DEPENDING ON THE SITUATION**.

By default the horizontal axis is derived from whatever there are more of, rows or columns, but you can choose yourself, either when you are creating the chart, or after you have created it.

5 Answers to activities

Activity 5
on page 8

There are several obvious things that you can do:

- cut down the amount of information you provide;
- slow down to a speed the listeners can cope with;
- focus on a small number of issues;
- organize what you are going to say so that it is easy to follow;
- check frequently to make sure your audience is keeping up with you;
- repeat and emphasize your key messages;
- use visual aids and handouts.

Activity 24
on page 42

Products A and B both suffer a dip in sales in May and October, and both show a significant rise in sales in July and from October to December.

Activity 25
on page 44

Products A and B show opposite behaviour in the first two months. Product A sales roughly double in February, but fall back slightly in March. Product B sales roughly halve in February and fall a bit further in March.

Activity 33
on page 62

Office packages typically have a variety of clip-art images that you can use to liven up your documents, reports or presentations, but take care with these: many are rather cartoon-like and if you use them too much or use them inappropriately your work may not be taken seriously.

Product photos and diagrams may well be available from the production department in your organization.

The Internet is a fabulous source of graphic images, but again care is needed. If you use an image found on the Internet it may be subject to copyright restrictions.

 # 6 Answers to the quick quiz

Answer 1

The main purpose of a briefing is to give information out and get information back.

Answer 2   When briefing people you don't know:

- don't assume your listeners know as much as you do;
- don't use language they might not understand;
- don't give them too much information too quickly.

Answer 3   The steps involved in planning and preparing a briefing are:

Step	Action
1	Draft the objectives
2	List the content
3	Design the structure
4	Prepare the visual aids and demonstrations
5	Have a rehearsal

Answer 4   You should design the main part of the briefing first.

Answer 5   Before you begin your briefing, you should check that:

- all your **VISUAL AIDS** are ready;
- the **EQUIPMENT** is set up and working properly.

Answer 6   Techniques for getting your message across include the following:

1 Repeat the central message at least once.
2 Speak loudly and clearly.
3 Keep it short and simple.
4 Be assertive rather than aggressive.
5 Use words and phrases that you are confident the team members will understand.
6 Check that they understand.
7 Use eye contact.

Answer 7   Feedback tells the original sender whether:

- the message has got through;
- action, if any, has been or will be taken;
- the purpose has been achieved.

Answer 8   The bars should be the same width.

Answer 9   A chart can be edited and formatted by right clicking on the chart as a whole or on an individual item within it and choosing from the menu options presented (Format chart, Format axis, etc.).

Answer 10   Pictograms present data in a simple and appealing way and for this reason they are often used in the media. However, pictograms are not appropriate if you need to give precise figures. You can use portions of a symbol to represent smaller quantities, but there are limits to what you can do.

7 Certificate

Completion of this certificate by an authorized person shows that you have worked through all the parts of this workbook and satisfactorily completed the assessments. The certificate provides a record of what you have done that may be used for exemptions or as evidence of prior learning against other nationally certificated qualifications.

superseries

Giving Briefings and Making Presentations in the Workplace

....

has satisfactorily completed this workbook

Name of signatory   ....

Position   ....

Signature   ....

Date   ....

Official stamp

Pergamon
Flexible
Learning

Fifth Edition

superseries

FIFTH EDITION

Workbooks in the series:

Achieving Objectives Through Time Management	978-0-08-046415-2
Building the Team	978-0-08-046412-1
Coaching and Training your Work Team	978-0-08-046418-3
Communicating One-to-One at Work	978-0-08-046438-1
Developing Yourself and Others	978-0-08-046414-5
Effective Meetings for Managers	978-0-08-046439-8
Giving Briefings and Making Presentations in the Workplace	978-0-08-046436-7
Influencing Others at Work	978-0-08-046435-0
Introduction to Leadership	978-0-08-046411-4
Managing Conflict in the Workplace	978-0-08-046416-9
Managing Creativity and Innovation in the Workplace	978-0-08-046441-1
Managing Customer Service	978-0-08-046419-0
Managing Health and Safety at Work	978-0-08-046426-8
Managing Performance	978-0-08-046429-9
Managing Projects	978-0-08-046425-1
Managing Stress in the Workplace	978-0-08-046417-6
Managing the Effective Use of Equipment	978-0-08-046432-9
Managing the Efficient Use of Materials	978-0-08-046431-2
Managing the Employment Relationship	978-0-08-046443-5
Marketing for Managers	978-0-08-046974-4
Motivating to Perform in the Workplace	978-0-08-046413-8
Obtaining Information for Effective Management	978-0-08-046434-3
Organizing and Delegating	978-0-08-046422-0
Planning Change in the Workplace	978-0-08-046444-2
Planning to Work Efficiently	978-0-08-046421-3
Providing Quality to Customers	978-0-08-046420-6
Recruiting, Selecting and Inducting New Staff in the Workplace	978-0-08-046442-8
Solving Problems and Making Decisions	978-0-08-046423-7
Understanding Change in the Workplace	978-0-08-046424-4
Understanding Culture and Ethics in Organizations	978-0-08-046428-2
Understanding Organizations in their Context	978-0-08-046427-5
Understanding the Communication Process in the Workplace	978-0-08-046433-6
Understanding Workplace Information Systems	978-0-08-046440-4
Working with Costs and Budgets	978-0-08-046430-5
Writing for Business	978-0-08-046437-4

For prices and availability please telephone our order helpline
or email

+44 (0) 1865 474010
directorders@elsevier.com